WRITTEN BY
RICHARD
BALKWILL AND A.J. WOOD WITH
THANKS TO TOM, THE ORIGINAL F.N. WHISKAS

ILLUSTRATED BY
HELEN WARD WITH THANKS TO
COMMANDER BOAZ
COHN BEAN FOR FELINE INSPIRATION

A TEMPLAR BOOK

Devised and produced by The Templar Company plc,

Pippbrook Mill, London Road, Dorking, Surrey RH4 1JE, England.

Designed by Mike Jolley

Encoded messages and Decoder supplied by OPSEC PLC - United Kingdom

Printed in Singapore

ISBN   1-898784-58-2

TEMPLAR

GATHER
YOUR WITS
ABOUT
YOU, FOR
MILTON'S MYSTERY
IS ABOUT TO BEGIN!
SEE IF YOU CAN
HELP HIM
SOLVE THE PUZZLES
IN THIS BOOK –
AND REMEMBER,
YOU HAVE YOUR
VERY OWN **MAGIC**
MAGNIFYING GLASS
TO HELP YOU!

M ilton the Cat needs to find a hidden treasure, but before he can start his search he needs to know what the treasure is! You can help him by solving the seven riddles or puzzles that you'll come across in the following pages. The answer to each one is an object that you will find somewhere in the accompanying picture. Once you've found it (and remember there may be more than one), look at it through your magic glass and part of a hidden message will be revealed.

You also need to find a key in each picture in order to discover seven hidden numbers. When you've gathered all the words and numbers together, see if you can work out what they are trying to tell you.

The answer will lead you back through the book to search for Milton's secret treasure with the help of your magic glass. On the way, if you look at the pictures carefully, you will come across all sorts of other hidden signs. Remember, anything marked with the sign of a fish is a red herring 🐟, put there to catch you out. Look instead for the sign of the cat's paw 🐾 - it's there to help you solve the final mystery! And if you get really stuck, just open the seal at the back of the book and all the answers will be revealed...

TWO GOLDEN RULES FOR GOOD DETECTIVES
1. Some hidden messages will be harder to find than others. **Be patient and careful when using your magic glass.**
2. If you can't find a hidden message, it may be because you are looking in the wrong place! **Don't be fooled by false trails and red herrings.**

IMPORTANT
Practise using your magic glass before you start this book. Lay your glass over the one printed here, colored side up. Make sure you press it firmly down onto the page. Now rotate it slowly round. Can you see the magic working? It will make a pattern of lines appear in the center of the glass before the hidden message finally pops into view.

There had always been Canfields at Canfield House. For six generations they had lived there, through sieges, plagues, floods, even fires! And the Canfields had always had a cat. Or so Milton, the latest in a long line of Canfield cats, thought. But one day all that seemed about to change...

The day in question found Milton lying, as usual, on the sofa, soaking up the sunshine. He wasn't paying much attention to the conversation going on behind him. But, as snippets of it drifted to him across the room, he began to take notice.
"I don't believe it!" Milton recognized the voice of Ben, the youngest Canfield.
"It's true. They owe half a million!" That was Jo, Ben's older brother.
"But what will happen to Canfield House?"
"Dad will have to sell - after all, it's the only thing we've got left that's worth anything," said Jo. "We're moving out next week - to an apartment in the city. And poor old Milton's going to live with Auntie Mabel..."
Milton couldn't believe his ears. Canfield House for sale! An apartment in the city!! Auntie MABEL!!!
Milton needed to think and think hard. There was only one place to go when thinking was needed and that was the attic, so he jumped off the cushion and padded up the stairs.

HERALDRY
THE ART OF
SYMBOLISM

THE MEANING OF
DREAMS
— CHAPTER III —
82

Up, up, up Milton climbed until at last he pushed open the door to his favorite room. The attic was full of all sorts of things - the relics of Canfield's past owners lay gathering dust in every corner. From his bed amongst a nest of old diaries and newspapers, Milton surveyed the mess of assorted household items that covered the floor and stretched from floor to ceiling.

Ancient children's toys, pots and pans, old paintings, battered suitcases, shelves of long-forgotten books - all of it part of Milton's home and all of it about to be sold.

"What a disaster!" thought Milton to himself. If only there was something that he could do to help. But of course that was out of the question. After all, he was just a cat. So, tired and anxious, Milton did the next best thing and fell into a deep and restless sleep...

From somewhere nearby Milton heard a voice calling him.
"Milton! MILTON! Will you wake up, you lazy, good-for-nothing bag of
bones." Milton blinked his eyes and was surprised to see an old black and
white cat standing before him. "Your Great-Uncle Furze N. Whiskas at
your service," said the old cat sternly. "I am here to help you save
Canfield House, don't y'know. Shame that you are such a miserable
moper and not worthy of my advice - but since you're the only cat here,
you'll have to do. So sit up, straighten your whiskers and listen."
Milton was too surprised to argue so he did just as he was told.

"The answer to all your problems is right here under your nose - you just
need to find it," continued Milton's Great-Uncle. "And to do that you
will need this..." he said, handing Milton what looked like an old rusty
magnifying glass.
"What am I supposed
to do with it?"
mewed Milton.

"Why, look through it of course," said Uncle Furze. "But you'll need to solve the puzzles first."

"What puzzles?" mewed Milton even louder.

"Don't worry," laughed Uncle Furze. "They'll find you! Now, if you'll just pay attention to my song, I'll be off."

With that, he unfolded a crumpled piece of paper and began to sing a strange caterwaul. As soon as the last note faded, Milton was astonished to find that both his ancient relation *and* the attic had completely disappeared! Instead, Milton was sitting amongst the green grass of a meadow. In the distance he could see a great castle. Knights in armor were jousting - a tournament was in progress...

A CATERWAUL
By F.N. Whiskas

"Go! Seven objects you must find, and far you'll have to roam.
Across the sea to foreign climes, but never far from home.
This ancient glass will help you find a message hidden there,
That added up will mean a prize to banish every care.
Things aren't always what they seem,
so read between the lines.
The answer's hiding somewhere there if you just read the signs.
And don't forget, where e'er you go, you must collect a key,
For only then can you unlock this magic mystery.
And finally, keep courage bold! Remember always that
You have a set of gifts to use
that come from being a cat!"

"M iaow!!" cried Milton in surprise, but before he could think what to do next a beautiful lady in a pointed white hat called to him.

"Take this to the Red Knight," she urged, giving Milton a white lace handkerchief. Milton looked down at the scrap of lace. Around the edge someone had embroidered a message:

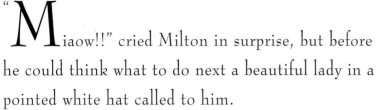

"Give Only Bold Looks at Every Turn!"

"Well I never," said Milton. "I've found a puzzle - or rather it's found me. Uncle Furze was right!" It didn't take Milton long to work out what the puzzle meant and only a little longer to find the first object, thanks to his feline climbing skills! And when he looked at his find with the magic glass, sure enough, there was the first part of the message. But Milton had no time to congratulate himself – for two snarling dogs started to chase him. So off he ran, across the meadow, through a gap in a fence, until finally he came to a door in a stone wall. Luckily it was ajar...

Rich   Ba
of York Ga in
Vain .

M uch to Milton's surprise, he found himself in the middle of a railway station! "I must be dreaming," he muttered. But the sound of barking behind him soon sent him scrambling for safety again. Dashing across the crowded platform, Milton dived headfirst into an open picnic hamper. No sooner had he done so when the lid slammed shut and Milton felt the basket being lifted up.

"Miserable mouselets!" cursed Milton. "Now I'll never find the next puzzle." Just then he noticed a curious label through a hole in the side of the hamper.

At first it just looked like a jumble of letters, but then Milton realised that it concealed four words.

"It's the second puzzle!" said Milton. Minutes later, he was so busy looking at the hidden message through the magic glass that he almost didn't notice that the hamper had been set down with a bump...

```
T H E P P B A
Z E W S S F C
I G K O O R L
Q U H S R A C
B X V I I E E
R E W J U J B
```

Gingerly Milton raised the hamper lid. He was looking out, not at the inside of a railway carriage as you might have thought, but at a busy kitchen. There was a table covered in food and a red-faced cook was shouting loudly in the background. "Bring me the milk! Boil the soup! Peel the potatoes!" Milton slipped quietly out of the hamper to take refuge beneath the kitchen table. But before he could begin to investigate further, plop, a huge dollop of sticky orange marmalade dripped from the tabletop onto his fur.

"How irritating," mewed Milton who disliked nothing more than marmalade. He retired beneath the table to clean it off and was even more irritated to discover that several bits of paper had somehow attached themselves to the sticky mess.

"Ah ha!" purred Milton looking at them. "A riddle!"

My first is in fin and also in fly.
My next's in the river, not the stream running by.
My third is in silver and also in sun.
And I glitter like treasure that somebody's won.
My last is in hungry and also in catch.
And for speed in the water I'm anyone's match.
My whole is a word that rhymes nicely with dish -
An unfortunate thought if, like me, you're a...

Milton sniffed the air. It took him only a matter of seconds to locate the third part of the message. But, just as he was congratulating himself, he heard the cook shout:

"Get that cat out of my kitchen!"
and he narrowly missed being hit by a flying rolling pin.

Red And
Indigo
Nicely
Brighten
Orange
Water

THE BUGLE'S
15th September 1879
Famous Painter
leaves for
England

Bolting through the kitchen door, Milton found himself surrounded by dense undergrowth. He was in the middle of a jungle. Lush plants grew thickly together. Beautiful birds squawked at him from the branches above. In the distance he could hear the sea. The whole scene looked strangely familiar, yet Milton couldn't think for the life of him where he had seen it before...

Then he noticed that the ground was littered with sheets of paper - maps, strange mathematical equations, pages from a diary.

One in particular caught his attention, for scribbled on it (in very bad handwriting) was another riddle.

Despite my name,
*   I cannot see,*
Yet everybody looks at me.
*   I have two hands,*
*   but not two feet.*
*   I have a face, but cannot eat.*
*   To find my name will take you time.*
And that's the purpose of this rhyme.

"Easy-peasy!" said Milton. Listening hard, it took him only a matter of seconds to find what he was looking for.

"Now to discover the fourth piece of the message," purred Milton, pulling out the magic glass. But, just as he was reading the hidden word, a terrible squawking from overhead made him jump and, with an almighty splash, he fell headfirst into the jungle stream.

Spluttering horribly, Milton felt himself being yanked upwards. Salt water stung his eyes and nose. "Miaow! Yeow, yeow!" he wailed, lashing out furiously. "Now that's no way to say thank you, pusscat," said a gruff voice and Milton looked up to see a great bearded man bending over him. Looking round, he seemed to be on some kind of ship. But Milton was too busy being miserable about his wet fur to be surprised by this latest turn of events.

"Welcome to *The Urma Bell*," said the bearded man. "We're going down now, about 40 fathoms. Should be there in no time. Oh, and here's your invitation. Don't lose it or they won't let you in."

Milton coughed out a mouthful of seawater as a lavish card was thrust into his paw.

"What! No riddle?" thought Milton, studying it closely. Then he had an idea and turned the invitation over. There on the back was a string of numbers.

12 15 15 11 6 15 18 20 8 5 21 13 2 18 5 12 12 1

Milton looked at the front of the card again.

"Of course," he said. But when he worked out the answer, he wasn't amused. "A fat lot of use when I'm already wet!" And, muttering crossly, he curled up for a nap beneath the control panel where it was warm and dry.

THE CO...

10th November 1879

Masterpiece
up for sale

Golden Afternoon

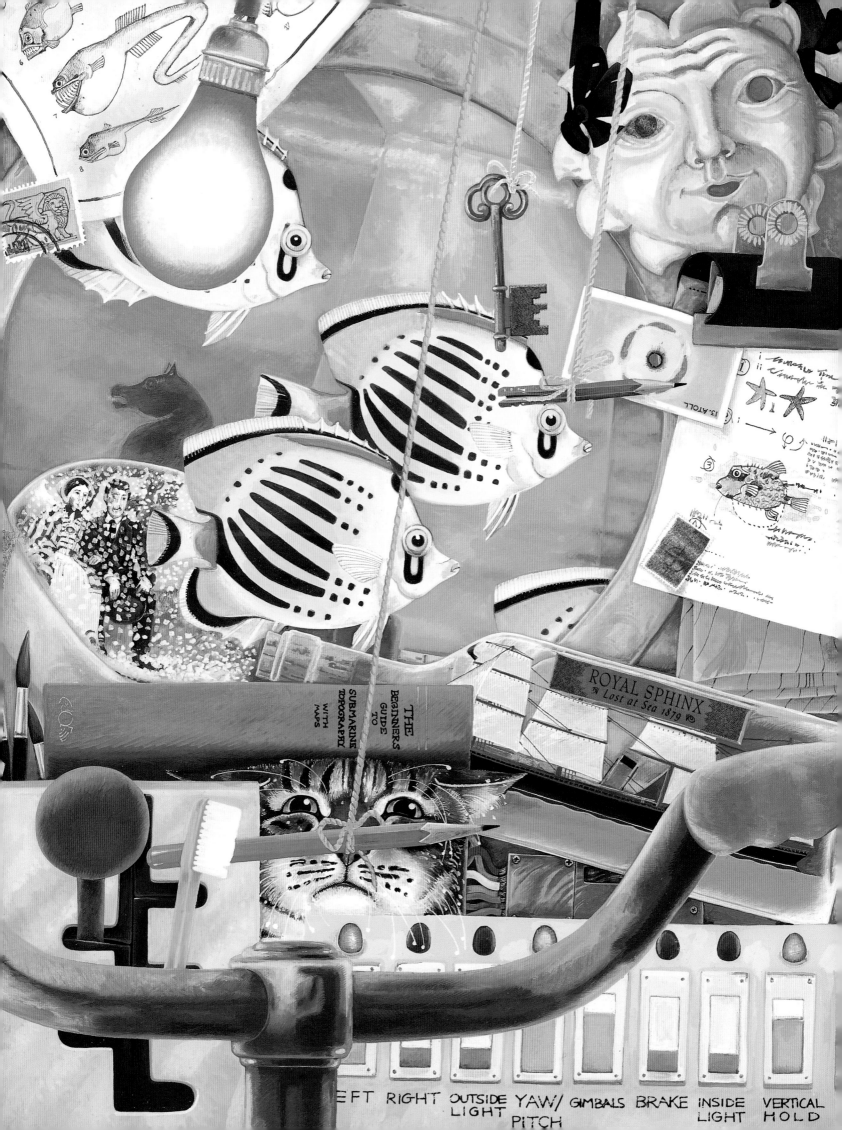

Milton woke with a start. It was dark. In the distance, he could hear music and laughter. Above him he could make out the outline of grand buildings with water running like roads in between them. There was no sign of the submarine or the bearded captain, but Milton still had his invitation. He crossed a tiny bridge and turned a corner. There, at the end of a narrow passageway, was a great square with a grand palace rising up on the far side. Everywhere, people in beautiful costumes were dancing and talking.

A man in a cat mask came over to Milton. "Whenever you're ready to leave, meet me over by the steps," he said, handing Milton a ticket.

BALLOON RIDES
(Cats go free)
H. COORB
PROPRIETOR

Just then the moon came out from behind a cloud. Something glinting in the dark shadows caught Milton's eye. He looked at the ticket again and purred contentedly for he could see what it was telling him to look for. Thanks to his excellent eyesight, it took him no time to collect the next part of the message. "That makes six. Now there's only one more piece to find, and I bet I know who can help me find it", said Milton excitedly, and he set off to look for the man in the cat's mask.

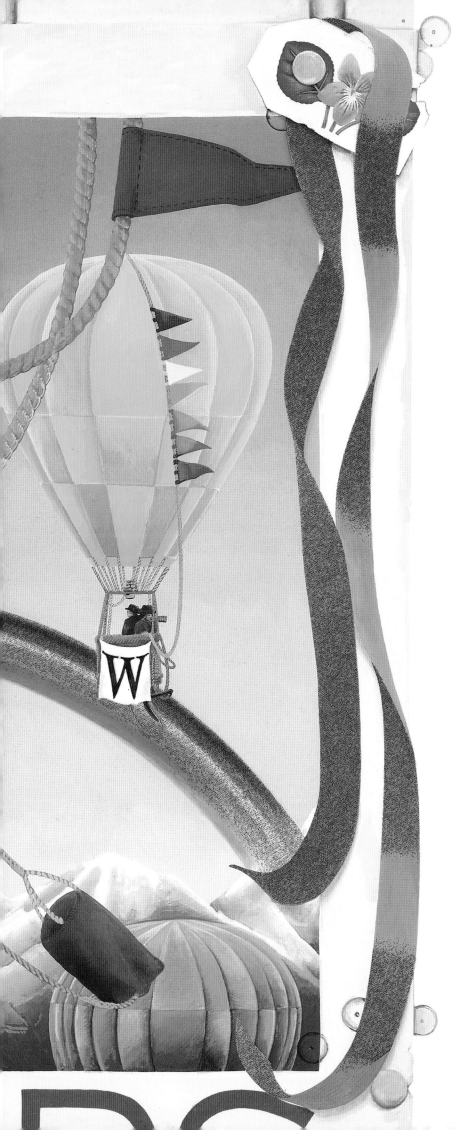

The basket creaked as the great balloon floated slowly through the rosy dawn. Milton was one of several passengers on Harry Coorb's morning balloon flight and, after several hours of drifting aimlessly along, he was bored. Yes, the scenery was beautiful, but all Milton was interested in was the seventh puzzle, the final object, the final part of the message, for without it the other bits made no sense to him at all.

He was sure that the puzzle was somewhere here but he had searched the basket and studied all the passengers to no avail.

Milton sat looking out of a hole in the side of the basket and thought hard. He thought of everything Great-Uncle Furze had said, about roaming far across the sea and using all the skills he had as a cat. Well, most of it had come true, except that the thing he was best at hadn't been of any use at all...

Just then one of the female passengers let out a piercing scream.

"Eeeeeeeek!" she shouted. "Get that thing away from me!"

"It's only a toy," laughed one of the men. "*Mus musculus*, introduced throughout the world from Europe if you must know."

But Milton didn't wait to hear the rest, for this was it - the final piece of the puzzle almost within his grasp. And he grabbed at it with both paws as it fell past him, reaching out into the cold morning air, stretching further and further in an effort to catch it, until he felt himself falling right out of the basket.

Down, down, down Milton fell, or rather floated, for strangely as soon as his paws closed around the final object the snowy mountains and colorful balloons completely disappeared. Instead, Milton found himself falling through a swirl of strange things - pieces of a jigsaw, a train ticket, a fresh brown hen's egg, brushes and paints, an alarm clock that was still ringing. All seemed strangely familiar, and as they twisted and turned before his eyes, he heard again his Great-Uncle's voice:

Tomorrow you may find the path that leads to finer weather!
Let seven keys show you the way to put the words together.
If you have done things properly and found the seven clues,
The only other thing to add is - always read the news!

Suddenly, the terrible truth dawned on poor Milton. Yes, he'd collected all seven clues, but the message still made no sense. And no wonder, for he'd completely forgotten to collect the seven keys! Now he'd never be able to solve the puzzle and save Canfield House. Unless, of course, there was someone who could help him...

CAN YOU
WORK OUT THE
MEANING OF
THE MYSTERIOUS
MESSAGE AND SO
HELP MILTON TO SAVE
CANFIELD HOUSE? IF YOU
THINK YOU KNOW WHAT TO LOOK FOR, GO BACK
THROUGH THE BOOK AND SEE IF YOU CAN FIND IT.
BUT BEWARE OF FALSE TRAILS!
AND, REMEMBER, THERE'S ANOTHER PUZZLE TO
SOLVE, TOO. SOMEWHERE WITHIN THE PICTURES
THERE ARE 22 HIDDEN CAT'S PAWS.
FIND THEM ALL
AND YOU WILL BE ABLE
TO WORK OUT
THE FINAL MYSTERY...

THE FIRST PUZZLE

So, how well did you do at being a detective?

If you are good at solving puzzles, you will have worked out that Milton's mystery message told him to look for a rainbow. There are lots of rainbows painted throughout the book, but all except one are marked with the sign of the red herring, put there to mislead the unwary. The rainbow Milton needs to find is on a painting in the attic, marked with the sign of the cat's paw.

If you haven't managed to solve the second mystery (which will explain why the rainbow painting is the answer to all Milton's problems), read the section over the page on MILTON'S SECOND MYSTERY. If you didn't manage to solve the first puzzle, here's how it works:

The answer to each of the seven riddles is an object. Here's how to work them out:

Castle scene:

"Give Only Bold Looks at Every Turn!"

If you take the first letter of every word printed in bold and put them together they spell GOBLET.

Station scene: There is a hidden message in the word box. It says LOOK FOR THE BASKET.

Kitchen scene: The answer to the riddle is FISH. (In fact, the fish in question is *Salmo gairdneri* - the rainbow trout - a fact that super sleuths may have deduced from the recipe pinned to the wall.)

Jungle scene: The answer to the riddle is WATCH.

Submarine scene: The invitation gives you the code you need to crack the secret message hidden within the string of numbers. It tells you that A=1, so B=2 and so on. If you use this code to translate the number code it says LOOK FOR THE UMBRELLA. Good detectives may have also noticed that both the Captain's name, *A.L. Rumble*, and the name of the submarine, *Urma Bell*, are both anagrams of the word umbrella.

Ball scene: If you look at the name on the card you will see that *H. COORB* is BROOCH spelt backwards.

Balloon scene: So to the final piece of the message! What do you think Milton would be best at? Why, catching mice of course! And that is just what *Mus Musculus* stands for in Latin. The final object you need to look for is a MOUSE.

T H E P B A
Z E W S F C
I G K O O L
Q U H S R C
B X V I A E
R E W J U B

Now look for the object in the picture (and remember there may be more than one!). Examine it with your magic glass and you will find part of a hidden message, marked with the sign of the cat's paw. You also need to look for a key in each of the seven pictures. Each key will reveal a hidden number. Put them all together and this is what you'll get:

Object	Message	Number
GOBLET	CAN YOU FIND IT?	7
BASKET	LOOK!	1
FISH	HIDES	4
WATCH	ANSWER	3
UMBRELLA	WITHIN	5
BROOCH	MILTON'S	2
MOUSE	A RAINBOW	6

If you read the words in order starting with 1, the message says:

"LOOK! MILTON'S ANSWER HIDES WITHIN A RAINBOW.
CAN YOU FIND IT?"

Beware of other hidden messages - they are only there to lead you astray.

The very sharp-eyed may have noticed these other helpful hints to the identity of the treasure concealed within the pictures:
• The words on the banner in the castle scene *"Richard Of York Gave Battle In Vain"* are a well known mnemonic (a set of words to help you remember something) for remembering the order of the colors of a rainbow - Red, Orange, Yellow, Green, Blue, Indigo and Violet. There are lots more mnemonics hidden in the pictures too - look at the images on the shields above the snarling dogs in the castle picture (Ring, Owl, Yak, Gryphon, Bear, Ibis, Volcano), or the items on the shelf above the stove in the kitchen. Look back through the pictures and see if you can find 6 mnemonics in total.
• Each of the seven scenes themselves reflect the colors of the rainbow - the castle is mainly red, the station is orange, etc. You should also be able to find the letter R in the castle scene, A in the station and so on, spelling out RAINBOW.
• In addition to the rainbows in every picture (there are 10 marked with a red herring; did you find them all?), there are many other things painted in rainbow colors - the snail's shell in the jungle scene, for instance. Look back through the pictures and see if you can find 8 "rainbow" objects.
• Super sleuths will have found two more hidden messages - in the ribbons at the side of the balloon scene that continue to swirl through the final picture of Milton falling. On the first is a simple message: "Can you work it out?" On the second is another riddle: "What bow can you never tie?" The answer is, of course, A RAIN*BOW!*
• Both the string of keys in the attic and the numbers on the sandbags in the balloon picture also feature the number sequence 7143526.

MILTON'S SECOND MYSTERY

So you found the one rainbow marked with the sign of the cat's paw - the one on the painting in the attic. But did you work out why this painting is the answer to all of Milton's problems?

If your answer is "No", the key lies in piecing together the clues marked by the 22 hidden cat's paws. The last line of the rhyme in the final picture should have helped you on your way:

"The only other thing to add is — always read the news!"

You see, Milton's mystery actually started long, long ago, way back in 1879 when Canfield House was the home of Lord Arthur Canfield, his beautiful daughter Lucy and her beloved cat, the well-know mouser Furze N. Whiskas. In the January of that year Lucy met the famous Austrian painter Frederich Notlim and a great romance ensued. By the April they had announced their engagement, but all was not to work out as planned. Frederich had arranged a grand exhibition to take place that Autumn in London, but Lucy was unable to travel with him since both she and her father had been struck down by a mystery illness.

Frederich set sail for England alone, one of many passengers on board the ill-fated *Royal Sphinx*. That night a great storm raged and *The Royal Sphinx*, battered by enormous waves and howling winds, went down with all hands. Frederich Notlim's body was never found and Lucy Canfield herself died not long after - some say of a broken heart.

Almost the last thing she did before she died was to buy Frederich's last painting - a portrait of them both that he had painted only that Summer, entitled *The Golden Afternoon*.

No-one knew that Lucy Canfield was the mystery bidder who succeeded in buying Notlim's last masterpiece - no-one, of course, but her devoted feline friend F.N. Whiskas. In her distress, Lucy hid the painting away in the attic where it remains to this day, one of the "lost" masterpieces of nineteenth-century painting and now estimated to be worth well over $1 million! A fine solution to Milton and his owners' problems indeed.

So how is the clever detective to discover the tragic story that lurks within the pages of this book? Why, by reading the news, of course!

Many of the cat's paws mark a series of newspaper headlines that, when read in date order, tell the sad story as follows:

Society Times: 15th April, 1879 - "English heiress to marry"
The accompanying picture shows a picture of Lucy and Frederich that also appears, labelled, on the wall of the kitchen.

Canfield Post: 1st August, 1879 - "Mystery illness strikes local household"
The accompanying picture of Canfield House also appears as a painting in the same scene, hanging on the wall in the attic.

The Bugle: 15th September, 1879 - "Famous painter leaves for England"
You may also have noticed that the accompanying picture shows Frederich Notlim and *The Royal Sphinx*. You can see *The Royal Sphinx* again in the submarine scene. It appears as a ship-in-a-bottle, together with "Lost at sea 1879".

Canfield Post: 16th September, 1879 - "Storm warnings for the coast!"

New Clarion: 16th September, 1879 - "*Royal Sphinx* lost at sea"

Society Pages: 18th September, 1879 - "Notlim mourned"

The Courier: 10th November, 1879 - "Masterpiece up for sale"
The accompanying picture shows the painting of *The Golden Afternoon* that appears, labelled, in the gallery window as part of the ball scene.

News Daily: 17th November, 1879 - "*The Golden Afternoon* sells to a mystery bidder."

Arts News: 3rd April, 1996 - "Early Notlim fetches $1 million"

The final explanation is to be found in the pages of Lucy's diary that provide part of Milton's "bed" in the attic:

"17th November, 1879. At last *The Golden Afternoon* is mine. I could not allow anyone else to own it, even though I can hardly bear to look at it myself - the last picture dear Frederich painted of us before he was lost to me. If only he had not left America! At least I have the painting. I shall keep it secretly to remind me of what might have been…"

In addition to the newspaper headlines and the diary entry, there are many other clues to the underlying story hidden within the book. Did you spot the ones listed below?

• The shelf of books above Milton in the opening scene has one volume entitled *Great Painters of Our Time - F. Notlim 1822 - 1879.*

• In the attic there is a painting of Lucy Canfield, labelled *L.C. 1858-1880.*

• In the kitchen, there is a drawer of letters addressed to "To Darling Lucy Love F.N" and also a picture of Lucy and Frederich hanging on the kitchen wall.

• In the background of the Ball scene, the gallery window shows *The Golden Afternoon* - complete with Lucy, Frederich and F.N. Whiskas.

If you look closely at the pictures, you'll find that either Lucy and Frederich or *The Golden Afternoon* itself appears, at least in part, on 10 occasions. Can you spot them all?

So, Milton's mystery is finally solved! But we couldn't leave you without a couple of further questions to answer. You will know by now that Milton's Great-Uncle Whiskas was the only one, apart from Lucy, who knew the whereabouts of the painting. But do you know the significance of the seven places that Milton went to in his dream? And also the connection between the painting and the seven objects that Milton had to find? IF YOU CAN WORK OUT THIS FINAL PUZZLE THEN YOU CAN TRULY CALL YOURSELF A SUPER SLEUTH WELL DONE!